WITH QUIET ARDENCY

With Quiet Ardency
Lianne M. Bernardo

First Printing: 2018

ISBN: 978-1-7750431-2-6

Most of the poems featured in *With Quiet Ardency* were written between 2016 and the beginning of 2018.

Note about the font: The font featured in the titles on both the book cover and at the start of each poem is based on my own penmanship (when writing in print).

To the man with the smile
that can light all four corners of the wind—
These poems you'll never read are for you,
faint stars hidden in the noise of night

6.

When did this feeling begin?
I no longer recall,
can no longer remember
a time when I did not feel what I feel.
Was it when I first heard your voice?
Or when we first exchanged glances
and I gave an awkward wave?
I knew I was in trouble even then,
that I've fallen into your eyes
and find I cannot make my way back out.

ll.

Words fail where they should thrive,
a faintness of heart instead takes over.
Panic arises as to how to fill the void
lest my mind implodes in anxiety—

Just put me out of my misery,
why don't you?

III.

Is this what going mad feels like?
    —the longing and the re·living and the waiting
    until you yearn to jump out of your skin,
    caged animal circling its iron prison
    —the smiling and the recollecting
    and the urge to throw up—
    guts and feelings
    and everything in between.

LV.

Is it possible
for the heart to beat
without feeling,
the ever-present thrum
of deep longing?

V.

Embracing a shadow
and searching for a smile
in unseen places...
Your presence eludes me;
fate, it seems, has cast
its meddling hand.
Heaven forfend these knotted feelings,
cloaked in confusion,
haunted by second-guesses.
Let the true ones be true,
let love come through.

VI.

Laughter—
all I can do is laugh.
Are you losing sleep
thinking of me,
just as I'm losing sleep
—losing my mind—
thinking of you?

VII.

Look up, look up,
look him in the eye.
They say the eyes are windows to the soul;
let him see you're interested in more—
how you wish to keep him smiling,
and hold him up when life is crashing down.
Show him you have a whole lot of love
and you're saving it for him.

VIII.

Please forgive me
    (My dear? Darling? My love?
    I don't know what to call you)
if I'm not always upfront,
if I don't look you in the eye,
and speak only of trivial nothings
    (Even I can't make sense of them).
The walls safeguarding my heart
are made of stone, piled metres high,
and my head can't make sense of you.
Maybe I merely amuse you,
maybe you're simply humouring me;
or maybe I'm just thinking too much
and this could be something special.
So please forgive me
if I take forever and a day
to knock down these walls,
to look you in the eye,
to weigh my words
    (But perhaps you know this already).

LX.

Attend to your face
for it reveals too much:
every anxiety,
every flicker of amusement.

And when you blush
you might as well light up
a neon sign above your head.

X.

My heart, take stock:
It's not always confusion,
heavy despair,
and shudders of longing.

XL.

I'm just meandering along
with my day-to-day,
night-to-night business,
and here you are
wandering into my dreams
even as you're nowhere in sight
in my waking life.

XLL.

Your name should be commonplace,
like a preposition or a ballpoint pen.
And yet with every mention,
every encounter on paper,
I immediately think of you—
but you're nowhere
and you're everywhere,
following me like a ghost
(or a guardian angel).

When will it stop?
When will your name ring normal?
Your name echoes on
and on
and on...

XLLL.

Passing glances at missed intersections
divided by glass, space, and thought.
Perhaps all is not lost:
refracted visions can be made whole.

XLV.

Prove to me you're not perfect,
that you bear a fatal flaw in your design.
For all signs point to canonization:
the kindest, the most generous, the most considerate.

Prove to me you're human:
that you have your bad days,
that you're not Superman.
But you're damn well close to one;
you leave me in awe.

XV.

Perhaps this is how it will always be:
a word and a laugh here and there,
paths crossing as often as a total eclipse,
a rare smile flashing as sudden as
    a meteor shower gone too soon.

Perhaps I can learn to be content with this.
Perhaps, perhaps...

XVI.

Looking at you now
(when I have the courage to look you in the eye)
drinking you in,
trying to memorise
every sharp angle on your face,
the slight crinkles around your eyes,
the way they gleam when you speak,
when you smile.

But my eyes cannot focus
and my brain cannot process
so I'll just have to keep looking at you.

XVll.

Stars:
if only I can pick them
off the blackened sky
and give them to you
scattered in a canvas
painted by my own hand.
Instead my words will have to suffice,
lift you onward and upward
to reach them, the starry canopy.

XVlll.

It's just a chair
with your winter coat draped on it
but I'd like to think it's your way
of getting closer to me.

XLX.

Moments re-lived
over and over until
they become as worn as
a folded piece of paper
shoved in a random pocket
of memories.

XX.

This modern love
is three-fourths comedy,
one-fourth romantic,
filled with hijinks, accidents,
and avenues of conversation not pursued
followed by long periods of absences
and mortified recollection.

XXI.

There is always something in my hands
passing along from me to you
linking us together like a chain—
a sheet of paper, an instrument, a phone—
when all I want to do
is run my hands along
the solid contours of your arms,
the curve of your lips,
the lines drawn around your eyes
when you break into a smile.

XXll.

Your name is synonymous with longing,
like the name of a far-off country
I yearn to explore.

Your name is like that of a prayer,
of all the things I wish to have,
a streak of light in the dark.

XXlll.

If only I can bundle the word "hello"
with every thought and feeling
I cannot seem to express
without everything else getting in the way.
If only "hello" could be our code word
to express how we feel deep inside.

XXLV.

Is it bravery or madness
at four in the morning?
I cannot tell;
there's no light in the sky then.

XXV.

I don't want you to be
some hurdle for me to leap,
some rite of passage to overcome,
a practice run before the final match.
I want you to be the first,
and the last,
and my only.

XXVL.

Thump, thump, thump—
The hammering of your name
across my heart continues.

XXVLL.

Your name is like
a prayer on my lips:
I say it without thinking
sometimes.

XXVlll.

I can no longer look up
into the night sky
and gaze at the few stars
shining through the haze of city lights
without thinking of you.

It's not a full tapestry
—bright lamps drown out the rest—
but I hold on to those few
twinkling little specks
as I recall how much you regard them.

XXIX.

My hands were once
dainty and pale and pliable.
Now they are covered in scars,
inflicted by some unseen enemy;
they itch and bleed with every bend.
I'm embarrassed to show
my hands to you.

XXX.

Ahh, to be a fool sick in love
with her head in the clouds
and her heart ten paces ahead
dictating her every move.

XXXL.

Shall I tell
the soft drift of snow
and the pouring rain
of my ardour for you?
They ought to understand;
after all, they fall
continuously to the earth
without a care in the world.

XXXII.

My feelings for you
fill my heart up to the brim
that should this vessel burst,
who will recover the remains?

XXXLLL.

This is some fresh form of madness,
not seeing you,
yet surrounded by your words,
your artefacts left behind.
There is no escaping you
—you linger in the backdrop—
and the only cure it seems
is to see your face again.
But it's out of my hands;
our paths seldom cross these days
and I'm left clinging
on to your words,
these unsuspecting relics.

XXXLV.

You have a lot happening
    in your life, I get it;
like a wayward satellite
    altering tidal waves
    without second thought,
    I'm merely a passerby.
But I wish to remain in orbit,
    close against your planetary gravity,
    not banished to the outer reaches
    of the cosmic dance.
But who has a say in this?
The stars are too distant
    to shout their input.

XXXV.

The mere sound of your voice
makes me laugh in delight
and blush in quiet joy.

XXXVI.

You occupy corners
of my heart
I did not know
even existed.

XXXVLL.

Your voice dips but
I still hear the words.
If I do not stop, it is not
because I don't want to—
busy world beckons and calls.
But I hear you;
I always hear you.

XXXVlll.

Holding your gaze is like
cupping one's hands as
the rain pours;
one tries catching the droplets
and holding on to the water
for as long as one can.

XXXLX.

And should I lose you
it will not be enough
to set me on fire
and scatter my embers
against the wind
for moonlight and stardust
also bears memories of you.

XL.

Longing for you
has been my constant companion,
something of a friend,
an item I always pick up
before I leave the house.

XLL.

The miasma of longing
that I cannot contain
has bloomed into purple flowers
—purple for the
self-inflicted bruises
of my own impatience.
They fall from my fingertips,
their bulbs threaten to burst anew.

XLLL.

If I write these words for you
—only for you
(though the whole world sees)—
will you recognise them,
recognise you in them?
Will you know the sender was I,
quiet though I am,
quiet though my feelings are?
Will you see them for what they are?

XLIII.

Is it too much of an ask?
Longing for your strong arms,
your heart against mine?
Like the stars yearn for night
and the copper seen for gold,
my ears yearn for your voice,
your eyes resting against my soul
day in, day out
for all time.

XLV.

You are not my only
source of poetry
but your absence is
felt at every turn,
at every empty space
where the words ought to roam.

XLV.

The things I long for:
—the stars in the sky
—the stars in your heart

XLVL.

Humour me
once more
with your smile;
the world is dark
without it.

XLVII.

Your absence is palpable
in the air;
it stops me in my steps,
knocks the oxygen out
of my lungs,
forces me to feel the
empty spaces where
my heartbeats were.

XLVlll.

I search for you
even in my dreams;
never far in my thoughts you lie
yet ever so slightly out of reach.

XLLX.

The warmth in your eyes,
the clarity in which they shine,
lends me the words
to string the poetry you
have stoked in my heart.

∠.

Minutes are not enough
to satisfy long absences.
They leave you wanting,
starving for more:
—more looks—
—more smiles—
—more now—
than any daydream or
memory could provide.

22.

My heart is brimming
full of you;
it overflows and spills
onto my hands, down my chest,
across my lips.

LLL.

You stole my words
as you stole my thoughts,
whisked them away in
the hole of your absence,
my heart chasing after you
into the darkness of night.

LLLL.

There is poetry to be had
in the depth of your eyes,
in the stretch of your smile,
in the weight of the silence
between us.

LLV.

I can't quite say you've
reached my bones
but your constant presence
in my mind
has entered my bloodstream,
a drug I can't quite wean off.

LV.

And yet my bones yearn
for your skin against mine,
some natural interception,
an inevitability of time.

LVL.

This uncertainty of movement,
this disciplined stillness at rest,
the searching and the
subconscious pull of orbit—
I know what this is now,
this unnamed feeling
—this ache for you.

LVII.

Forgive my eyes:
they seek to protect me,
hide the depths of feelings inside.

Forgive my speech:
the inane ramblings,
the struggle to connect.

Forgive me, forgive me,
I'm a mess of emotion
—I want you to see me—
—I want you to want me—
but I fear
I'm lost in the plot,
I'm out of my depth.

Forgive me.

LVlll.

Under some half-baked moon
masked still by the darkness of night,
I long for you with a feeling
too foreign yet too delicate
to form into words.
Like a wind dispersing the
last mounds of leaves
making way for hardened frost,
my longing shifts form
but the feeling remains:
the wanting, the desiring,
the dreaming.

LLX.

Beloved, what passion runs in your veins?
What breaks the stillness of those ethereal lakes.
that sends currents against those waters?
What form do those busy-body heron take
as they dip into clear mirrors
upsetting the glass back to liquid
against the paleness of dawn?
Passion is such:
—a foreigner
—a disruptor
—a pulse against the calm.

∠X.

Your heart bears its own gravity
that draws me in
regardless of how it seems,
despite of all the complications.

—There I lie, in your orbit.

LXL.

And so it is again
that I continue to long for you
    from afar, silent as I am
for I have neither the tools nor the skill
to draw you closer,
to spill all I hold next to my chest
upon your lap,
your open mouth,
those raised eyebrows.

LXLL.

Red was never my kind of colour
until I met you.

LXIII.

I am a blue girl:
crystal as the sky,
deep as the sea,
cold as the snow coming down.
But because of you
I am awash in red.

LXLV.

The days are long
and our paths lie wide
apart, not touching,
not even close.
But all I see is your smile,
your perfect, open smile.

LXV.

Here, I offer you my chest,
this basket in which my heart lies,
blood red roses blooming hold,
these sacks called my lungs
that breathe in your scent,
your words—
They lie before you, an offering
wholly my choice.

LXVI.

And if I am wrong,
dare I burn every memory
associated with you?
Every song and every poem
in a funeral pyre
side by side with
every hope of us there is—
Would I be brave or
foolish enough to see
such despair through?

LXVll.

And so my feelings for you remain
a bouquet made of words settled
on paper that you will never read.

ABOUT THE AUTHOR

Lianne M. Bernardo is from Canada. She has previously written for high school and university publications, online e-zines, and Youth Speak News at the Catholic Register whilst accumulating a stack of unpublished content ranging from novel-length stories to poetry.

You can follow her on Instagram at *@shallibeapoetinstead*

ALSO BY THE AUTHOR

Shall I Be a Poet Instead?

Of Frost and Fury: Poems Written in the Land of Volcanoes and Giants